SMALL GRASS

Poems by Jacqueline Gabbitas
Artwork by Frances Barry

First published in 2014
by Stonewood Press
97 Benefield Road, Oundle PE8 4EU
Tel: 0845 456 4838
books@stonewoodpress.co.uk
www.stonewoodpress.co.uk

All rights reserved
Poems © Jacqueline Gabbitas, 2014
Artwork © Frances Barry, 2014
The author and artist assert their moral rights to be
indentified as the originators of this work

ISBN: 978-1-910413-00-5 (Paperback)
ISBN: 978-1-910413-01-2 (Hardback)

Distributed by Central Books
99 Wallis Road, London E9 5LN
Email: orders@centralbooks.com
Tel: 0845 458 9911

Printed and bound in the UK by Berforts Information Press,
King's Lynn, Norfolk

Designed and typeset in Sabon 10.5pt/12.5pt
by www.silbercow.co.uk

Acknowledgments

Jacqueline would like to thank the editors of the following magazines and anthologies in which some of these poems have appeared (some in different versions): *Long Poem Magazine*, *Poetry Salzburg Review*, *Staple*, *Artemis Poetry* and *Forward Book of Poetry 2010* (Faber, 2010). She would also like to give special thanks to Mimi Khalvati for her support and mentoring. Jacqueline received an Arts Council England Grant for the Arts to work on these and other grass poems, many of which were started during her Hawthornden Fellowship in 2009.

We would like to thank everyone who supported our #smallgrassfund campaign.

Small Grass *is a sequence drawn from a book-length poem by Jacqueline Gabbitas called* The Book of Grass.

For Mimi

Contents

Oxygen	9
Ground breaks for the coming of spring	10
Grass sings to her roots	13
Grass speaks at the foot of Volcano	15
Welcoming the burrs	16
Grass answers Mountain about her time of dying	19
Tall standing	21
Grass looks out over the short field	22
Grass eavesdrops at a church window	23
Armour	24
Grass sleeps and dreams of horses	27
Grass discovers metempsychosis	28
Red Thread	30
Grass laments the loss of light	31
Grass listens in awe of Wisent's morning song	35
Grass honours the low cloud	36
The finding and losing of grass	38
Notes	41
Supporters	44

SMALL GRASS

Oxygen

As there is sun, there's life.
As god speaks, there's life too.
And I grow,
And trees grow.
And algae has always grown.

As there is rain, there's life.
As god weeps, there's life too.
And I breathe,
And trees breathe.
But algae is holding its breath;

For as there's a world, there's an end.
As god sees, algae sees too:
A boiling land,
A burning sea.
And the air stripped out and empty.

Ground breaks for the coming of spring

My eyes are blind.
Everything, all beasts and birds,
all things that prey, are preyed on,
know how blind my eyes are, how
I find sun and sky by inheritance.
This they knew when they came to be.

I am passing through earth, passing
the souls of animals who nod
when my eyes (like a newborn worm)
seek them out for guidance.

My world has been glacial
and all I had was the roar of god,
then the small click of ice breaking.
My world has been burning,
and all I had was heat and carbon:
light surrounding. Until the ash.
I have known all states of things.

Each year I break through blind
to open my eyes for the sun, sky,
for the bridge of leaves above trees;
the creatures sleeping newly beneath them.

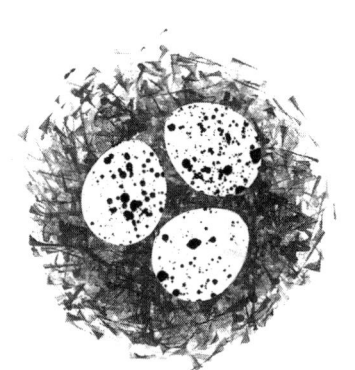

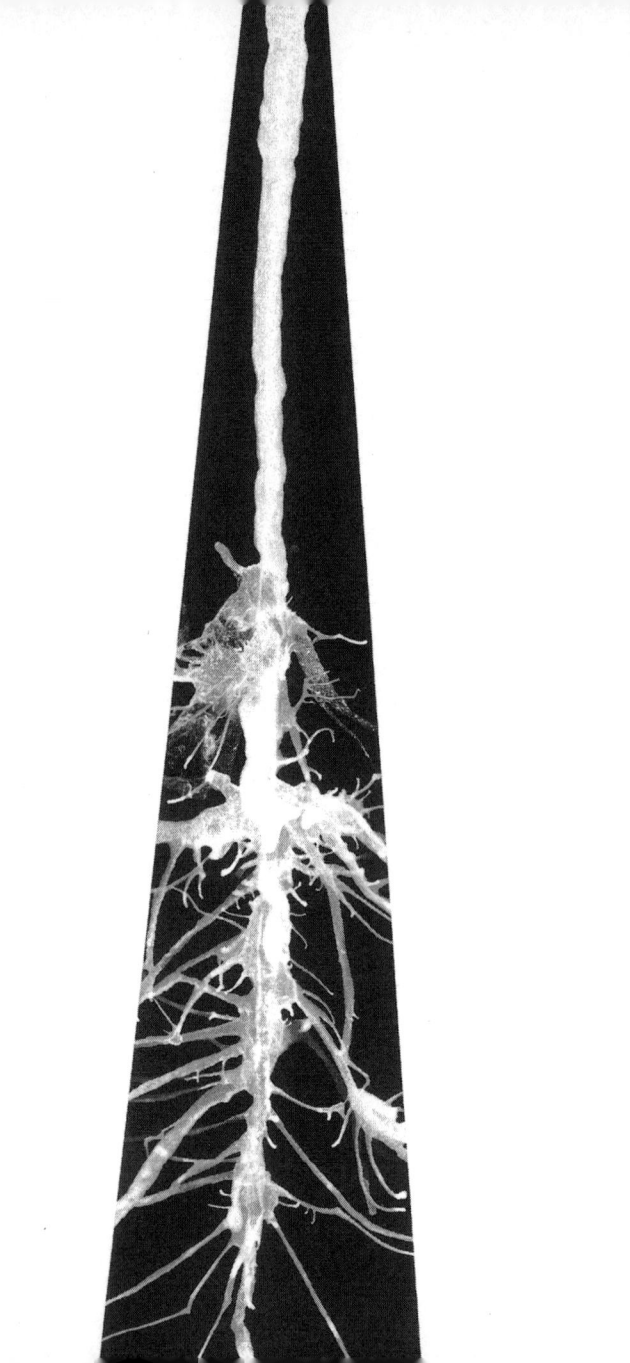

Grass sings to her roots

Man thinks these are the colours
of air and water, of light and freeing,
but before this they were ours:

our blades are green, our lowly stems
the red of poppies, pink of damask,
our rhizomes white as redemption.

And you, my loves, are palest yellow
like the long memory of sunlight
from a rainbow on a glacial floe.

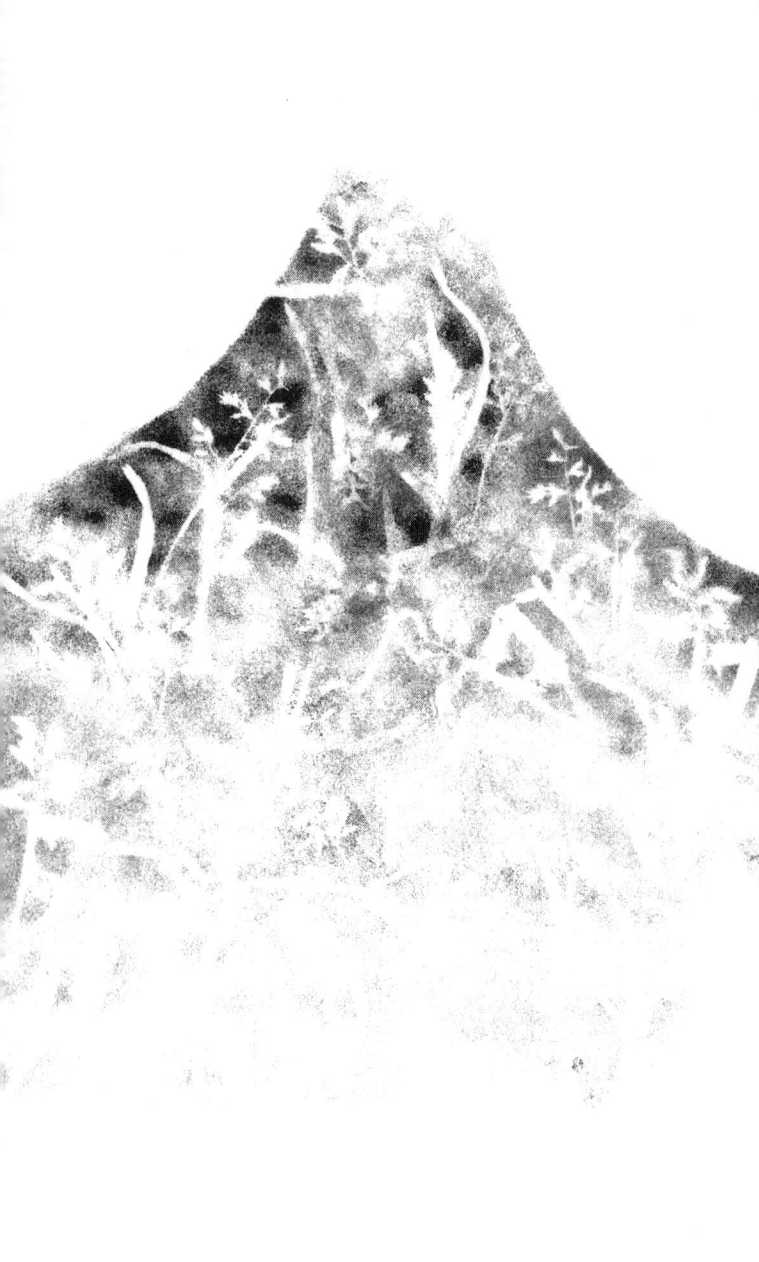

Grass speaks at the foot of Volcano

Haaauuuummm first, then shhhhhhhhh.

I don't pretend to understand him when
he says these things – but then I don't need to.
Why he thinks I can't speak, I can't tell you.
He hears me often, singing over miles.

Haauuuummmmm. Hauuuuummmm.

I leave him gifts beneath his lava glass;
pretty seeds and blossoms, something
for him to look at later when I'm gone
(something small for him to think about).

Sssshhh he learned from me –
I can't remember when – he liked
its simpleness, the way it almost capped
his anger. He's calmer now, I promise you.

Haauuuummmmm. Hauuuuummmm.

Welcoming the burrs

Let me take the seed that is your heart
and lungs, your promise of continuance,
and protect it from both grub and rat tooth.

Let me wear it! Jewel, brown as god's
horns, red as his blood, as the issue of man
in the war fields and deserts.

Let the seed be smooth for me, and shine
at night like the owls' eyes, never meagre
against the radiance of the moon.

Let me bathe it in the earliest dew,
warm it beneath the habit of the sun.
Let me give it to the earthworm's track.

Then, let it shrivel to a nub as close
to death as life. Let it wait out frosts,
the promise of snow, the winter droughts,
the uncertainty of if or how it will grow.

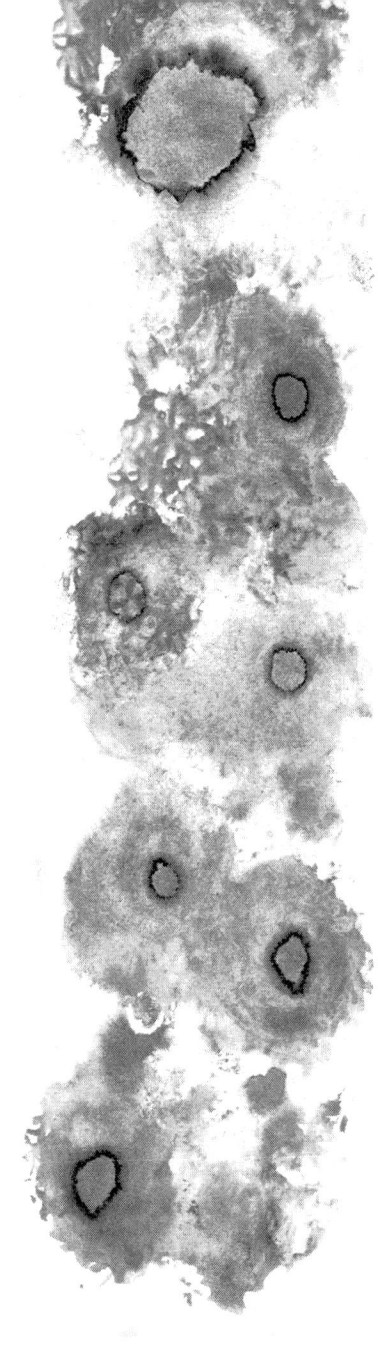

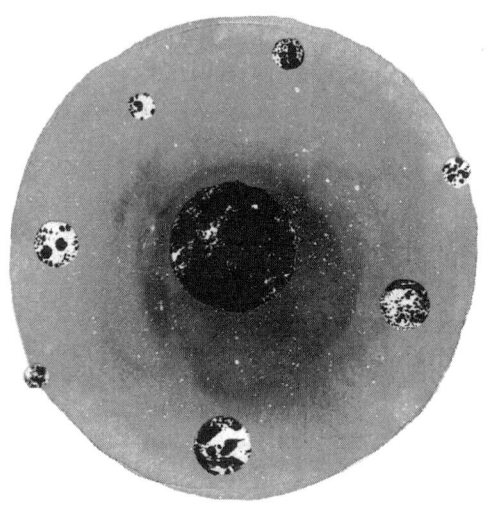

Grass answers Mountain about her time of dying

Trees, shrubs, ferns, grass; we stood
as neighbours and watched your birth
in fire, in molten mass – convulsion!

We each of us agreed you were glory,
even as we saw in you our endings:
the burgeoning and diminishing of cells,

the struggle for breath with no hope
of medicines but the small evolutionary
changes we could grab back from our fibres.

In his heaven above the withering trees,
god looked across and marvelled
at your new-born stone, stone of sediment

and the carcass of the sea and the ocean
– it sucked the very carbon from the air –
and he whispered in my ear, *grass*

you must evolve; look to the stars, imitate
the blackest hole and draw in all life.
Mutate, grass, mutate to survive.

Tall standing

I grew straight as a line between earth and sun,
and cast my long shadows over the apes
whose ambitions were no longer in the canopy.

I'd protected them in their apeness,
dappling their fur from the eyes of other apes,
from the rough tools and teeth of other apes.

And they were lovely then – short-stunted,
picking fleas from the creases round their eyes;
knees calloused; chattering in the darkness.

Did god whisper in their stubby ears: *Rise up!
Stand up over grass and I will make you man?*
Did he want me to befriend them?

I grew tall in the same way as light, but the apes
were no longer sustained by my protection.
– Who but god knew of the muscles in their hind legs,

their curiosity for the way of living
in the horizon of trees, their thirst for balance?
– And so an ape-child listened and rose up.

Standing, she saw it all: bloodied teeth and claws,
a future hairless and looking to be clothed,
mouths filled with words. Hands with tools.

Grass looks out over the short field

I strop my edges,
blade against green blade.

I've known many blades; some
fired from minerals, cooled by rain.

Always honed; taking me down
at the stomach, the neck, the knees.

From where I lie, I see man walking,
his legs sheathed in green.

I strop my edges. Soon, they'll cut through
fabric, the tissue beneath.

Grass eavesdrops at a church window

If man would put his ear to this glass
he'd hear my voice – my colossal reed

singing to my stems, my roots, amassing
my flower-heads, broadcasting seeds.

Armour

It would take the lens of a raindrop to see my armour –
and who would get that close? And who would think to?

Call it teeth, call it battleaxe, call it blade. When you bite me,
beware – I've seen the mouths of ancient horses bleeding.

I've worn blood like you wear a coat. It nourished me.
I've been eaten and shat out – battleaxe, blade and all.

Reptiles, mammals. They ate for months and died *en masse*;
their guts too infant, teeth too sharp to be useful.

I wept, then strengthened my armour. Waited
for the creatures who grew long hind teeth, and stone ones.

Grass sleeps and dreams of horses

The horses come back.
Black. Their mouths are bridled.
Their shins lacerated from my edges.

Field becomes desert.
I am under here, three, four fathoms
of sand. And the horses come back.

Desert becomes ice-desert.
I am seed and chaff in the melted core,
and man, face like a horse, looks down.

Ice-desert becomes town.
I am on the brow of a hill. A horse walks.
Her head hangs limply from her neck.

Grass discovers metempsychosis

It was the trees started it. It was the trees.
They said man first chose a sapling each,
barely from the seed: oak-woods, mahoganies.

Man stood by a river and stooped to drink.
Some called the river death and others life,
but always for man it was forgetting.

Yet the trees would remember. A hundred years
flooded by and the memories seeped in.
A hundred more and the memories strengthened:

I was an archer; a legionary.
I was a farmer; a herder of goats. I died, penniless.
I died with wine in my belly and water in my lungs,

I died singing to a woman I had no call to.
I died with sores under my arms and breath burning.
I was never let to be born.

But the trees only started it. Man looked around
and chose nightingales, otters, lions, teachers, kings.
and all the flowers – the small man who chose flowers –

fritillaries, roses, nightshades, forget-me-nots, lilies.
But the first chose trees: long lives, stationary.
None chose mayflies, none grasshoppers, none grass.

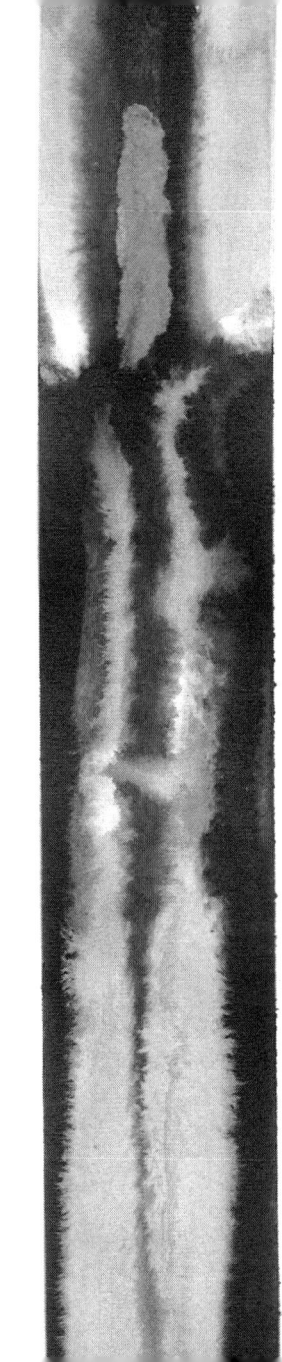

Red Thread

I cover Earth like a poultice, yet
am at a loss to find the medicine
that will cure her. As the virus is to man,
man is to Earth. He is snow mould, red thread!
Dwarf bunt! Loose smut! I could go on.

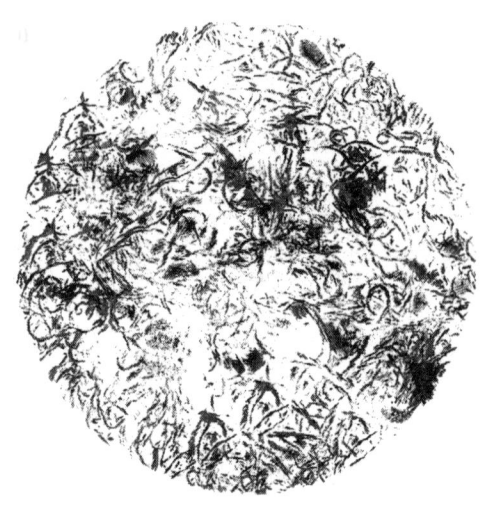

Grass laments the loss of light

All that is eaten is diminished.
All that is loss is vast.
Sun is vast yet diminished.

The days grow long and short.
They have always done. Even so.
They deceive us more than ever.

Man says everything's diminished,
nothing is lost. But where's the light?
A stripped field darkens before time.

A stone on a beach cools before time.
Fish swim deeper and evolve.
Mosquitoes live in tunnels. Evolve.

I am eaten. Sun is eaten.
We are both of us diminished.
Neither has the strength to speak.

And, robbed of its luminescence,
even the plankton of the rivers
and of the seas shrivels.

Grass listens in awe of Wisent's morning song

There are sounds more mellifluous than this,
and to list them is like counting the droplets
of rain that fall on her hairy head, the crystals
of ice on each of my blades. Her voice
carried on waves in the normal manner of sound
is nothing remarkable, but her song…
there's no hint of the *hlowan* of cattle,
of what her horns and the fatty mass
of her hide suggests. Her song is frozen
as the snow powdered on the lashes
of each sorrowful eye that saw
the rapid extirpation of her kind.

As the sun rises, she breathes out twice
and the landscape listens. She's haloed
in a history given her by man. She's haloed
in a light given her by god and sun and low cloud.
Snort and grunt and the easy bellow
of a greeting to the frozen earth, frozen sky –
this is the way she talks to the world. She is
the world. On the morning mist her breath,
her breath in sunlight is a prism, crepuscular,
escaping from a body hulked in blackness.
The blue sky – it is an outline to the meat of her.

Grass honours the low cloud

With seed and blade,
with root and rhizome,
with ears and eyes,
I lie down as you ascend:
a gathering of water,
a blanket warm
and barely penetrable.

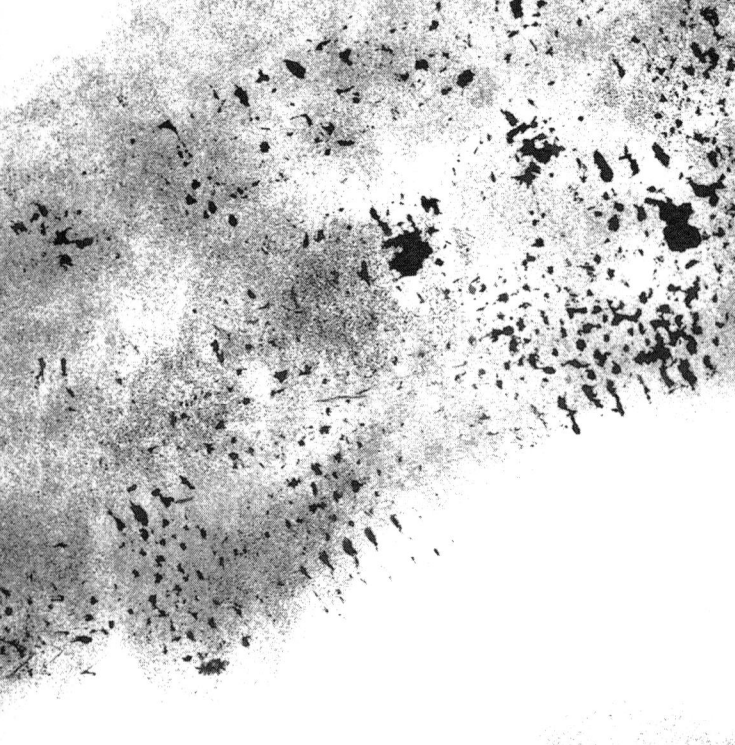

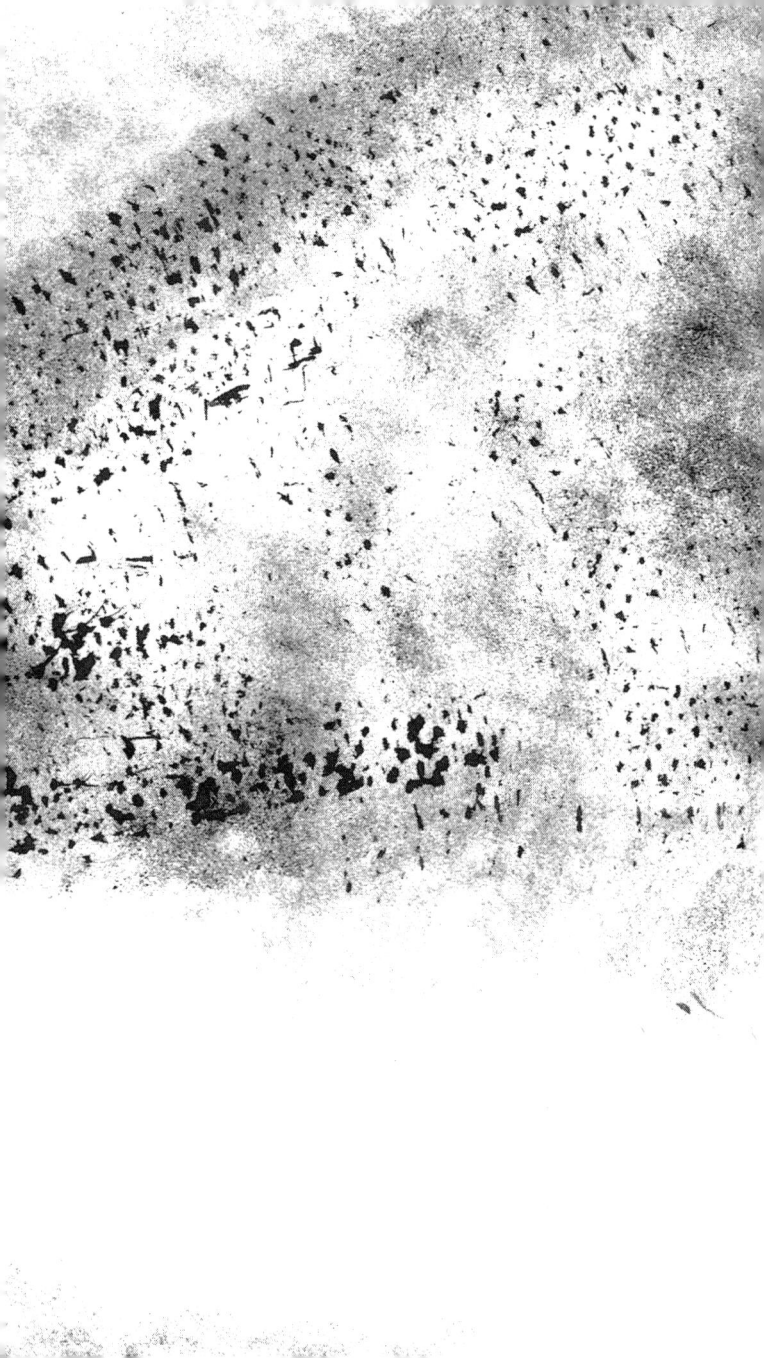

The finding and losing of grass

Before the snows came I blossomed;
a small act for a large season.

Tiny as the springtail, and as eager
to take the breeze, I opened up

– my head a rope of silken flowers,
yearning to be seeded.

The seeds came, the seeds went, my flowers
already ended.

But when the snows came they blossomed
still in their dead-heads.

And man that was woman saw me, stooped
and broke a single stem.

She was pleased with herself,
pleased with the way she made me fetish.

On the path to her dwellings
I slipped free of her pocket's tyranny.

If she mourned the loss,
I took it as no concern of mine. How am I lost?

In the deeps of this season
my dead-head will not be kept. I am gone.

NOTES

The artwork throughout *Small Grass* is made using inks and crayon, in part using collage, rubbing and frottage.

Oxygen: Algae and phyto-organisms are a natural carbon sink and produce approximately 25% of the oxygen in the Earth's atmosphere.

Grass answers Mountain about her time of dying: In order to survive the formation of sedimentary limestone, which could rapidly extract carbon from the atmosphere, grass evolved a system of channels in its blades that would extract carbon more efficiently.

Armour: As vegetation draws up water it transforms the silica mineral into microscopic barbs that it uses for protection. This evolutionary step is thought to have contributed to the extinction of many species of prehistoric mammals and reptiles.

Grass sleeps and dreams of horses: Ice core samples from Antarctica have uncovered grass seeds millions of years old.

Grass discovers metempsychosis: The transmigration of the human soul from one person to another or to another species. In *Republic,* Plato describes men and animals at a place of judgment choosing the form they wanted to return as. They then drank from the River Lethe and their souls left for their new births.

Red Thread: Red thread and the other expletive-like nouns in this poem are diseases of grass.

JACQUELINE GABBITAS' poetry has been published in magazines and anthologies including *Poetry Review*, *The Forward Book of Poetry* (Faber & Faber, 2010) and *Entering the Tapestry* (Enitharmon Press, 2005). Her short collections include *Mid Lands* (Hearing Eye, 2007) and *Earthworks* (Stonewood Press, 2012). She has read at The Oxford Times Literary Festival, The Poetry Library in London, and for BBC Radio 3's The Verb. Jacqueline is co-editor of Brittle Star magazine and the Marketing Manager for Writing East Midlands. www.jacquelinegabbitas.net

FRANCES BARRY studied Fine Art at Brighton Polytechnic and Royal Academy Schools. She is a freelance illustrator and author, and has worked extensively for the children's publisher Walker Books, as well as for Little Angel Theatre, London Underground, Gallery Five, Battersea Dogs' Home and the Charleston Trust. Frances is currently researching a public art project for Tate Enterprises. She is also studying puppetry and puppet making in London. www.francesbarry.com

Thank you to everyone who contributed to our Small Grass campaign. The names listed below are from supporters who chose perks from our campaign that included publication in *Small Grass*:

Anne Stewart, Caroline Natzler, Francoise Harvey, Gavin Jones, Hearing Eye, Hylda Sims, Kathryn Maris, Lee Marshall, Mary Dawson, Mimi Khalvati, Paul Blake, Paul Finlay, Pippa Hennessy, Sarah Parkinson, Sarah Passingham, Sarah Pickstone, Valerie J Gabbitas, Valerie Josephs and all our anonymous contributors.

This artists' chapbook was created to raise funds to contribute to Stonewood Press's growing list of new writing and emerging writers. Jacqueline and Frances donated their time and work to produce *Small Grass,* and all profits from the sale of this book go directly to Stonewood to support new writing.

http://smalllgrass.wordpress.com
#smallgrassfund

Other Stonewood Press titles:

Hoad and other stories by Sarah Passingham
Earthworks by Jacqueline Gabbitas
Stone and the Flower Dragon by JG Parker (ebook)
Dark Peak: The First Elemental by JG Parker
Notebook in hand: New and Selected Poems
by John Rety
Said and done: New Writing from Brittle Star
edited Louisa Hooper, Jacqueline Gabbitas,
David Floyd and Martin Parker, with a foreword
by Maureen Duffy

www.stonewoodpress.co.uk